Discovering Ezekiel

A Bible Excavation

by

Tam Raynor

Other books in this series by this author:

Discovering Leviticus

Discovering Deuteronomy

Other books by this author:

A Cross Examination

The Noble and the Dreadful: an Investigation of Bible Based Women

Spiritual Discoveries: One Soul's Search

Dove on a Barb'd Wire (a biographical novel)

Mzungu Expressions (autobiography of a missionary)

Africa Seen (short prose of personal experiences)

Search the Word Puzzles: Proverbs

Search the Word Puzzles 2: Ecclesiastes

Search the Word Puzzles 6: Acts

A-Ha Moments in the Book of Matthew (also Mark, Luke, John)

To the Acropolis and Beyond (from a trip Tam took)

Blue Boo and the Coo (a children's book illustrated by Tam)

Copyright © 2014 Tam Raynor

Updated 2024

Published by Raynor Shine Books

Cover design by Tam Raynor

Front cover photo: Ruins of Knossos, photo taken by Tam Raynor

Internal graphics based on Microsoft Word Clip-art, reworked by Tam Raynor

Fonts used: Times New Roman, Tempus Sans ITC, Calibri

All rights reserved.

ISBN-10:1494344025
ISBN-13:978-1494344023

DEDICATION

I dedicate this book to Jehovah God, who has mercy on me, a sinner, reviving me to life, when I inadvertently 'cross over' into the 'dead zone' of sin or apathy. May He always be ready to send me someone brave enough to preach the words of life.

CONTENTS

	Acknowledgments	i
	Introduction	1
1	Who Should I Talk To?	3
2	The Watchman	9
3	The Arrogance	15
4	The Idol of Jealousy	21
5	Profit or Prophet?	27
6	Shepherds and Wolves	33
7	This Groom is a Special Kind of Lover	39
8	Straying and Staying	45
9	Is Sin Inherited?	51
10	The Desire of My Eyes	57
11	Sooner or Later	61
12	The Grand Revival	67

ACKNOWLEDGMENTS

I thank a certain Israelite priest
captive in a foreign land
who had several out-of-body-experiences
who had several visions
who had a living God's words personally spoken to him
even though he wasn't especially desiring to be a deity's mouth piece
to a people who could care less
about hearing news from the God
that they didn't really
didn't honestly
didn't truly believe in

INTRODUCTION

Once, after having believed that prophesy only foretold the future, I discovered that in the Bible, only a few of the books of prophesy actually dealt with the future. Many of the Bible's prophets just ranted, raved, and condemned people, using poetic language! I never could get much out of reading those books until some New Testament passages caused me to "re-think my thinking."

Peter, in his second letter, said that no prophesy comes from human power, but instead, prophecies are messages that come straight from God, through the Holy Spirit, using humans as His pen and paper (2 Pet. 1:20-21). Peter later states that we must remember the words that the ancient prophets had spoken, and we must remember the commandments of Jesus spoken by the apostles (by the way, *apostles* means *ones sent,* as in a fleet or an embassy, 2 Pet. 3:1-2). Peter clumps Jesus' commandments, the apostles' teachings, and the Old Testament prophets into one group, leading me to consider the fact that prophecy has to do with all kinds of subject matters, not just foretelling the future.

While reading the books of Isaiah, Jeremiah, Ezekiel, and Daniel, I confirmed in my mind that the people in my country, and in the world today, are not any different from the people in Old Testament days. In addition, my eyes opened up to the vivid, colorful, verbal descriptions that God painted on the canvas of the Bible, skillfully using expensive brushes like Isaiah and Ezekiel to produce His own self portrait.

Ezekiel's book proves to be an extremely illustrated, graphic, and explicit writing; describing what God actually thinks and feels about apostasy and sin. Ezekiel does not beat around the bush, and he absolutely does not sugar-coat anything. It seems like God must have reached the end of His rope, and He wanted His thoughts to be unmistakably clear to His humans. God made Ezekiel just "flat out say it like it is," even to using extreme, vivid images.

I invite you to come with me and carefully dig through this stimulating, ancient manuscript. Together, we'll make discoveries about:

- inheriting or not inheriting sin
- being, or not being, accountable for someone else's life and choices
- whether or not preachers and prophets of God are infallible
- whether or not we can fall from grace
- what God really feels about people who stray from His words
- what it means to come back to life
- and much more…

Hold onto your pith helmets! Grab your picks and shovels! These lessons will be terribly dangerous to your Evil Lower Nature, and will be fraught with ancient curses; but if you can brave the dangers, you'll find treasures like you have never seen before!

I charge you in the presence of God and of Christ Jesus...preach the word...
1 Tim. 4:1, 2

LESSON ONE
Who Should I Talk To?

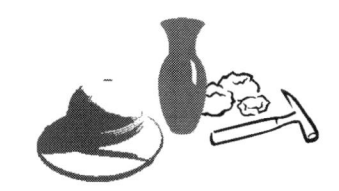

Brief Introduction: Ezekiel 1:1-3

1. What was Ezekiel?

2. Where was he living?

3. Exactly when did the *hand of the Lord* come upon him?

4. Ezekiel chapter 1 resembles what New Testament book? _____

   a. What does this resemblance tell you about the God of the New Testament?

5. Should we, today, pay attention to the words of Ezekiel? Explain.

Fill in the blanks (make changes depending on the Bible version you're using): **Ezekiel 3:11** (ESV)

"And go to the _____, to your _____, and speak to them and tell them, "Thus says the _____, whether they _____."

Questions: Ezekiel 1-3

1. In 1:28, what did Ezekiel do when he saw the *glory of the Lord*?

2. In Ezekiel 2:1, what did the Lord tell Ezekiel to do and why?

3. Do you think that God desires to speak to you? Why or why not? (Give some New Testament verses on this subject, for example: Mark 6:34 or John 20:30-31)

4. In Ezekiel 2:3-4, to whom was God sending Ezekiel and what kind of people were they?

5. What was Ezekiel supposed to say to them?

(continued next page)

6. In Ezekiel 2:5, 7, when was he to talk to the people?

    a. Explain the similarities between these verses and 2 Timothy 4:2-4.

7. Read 2:6…How can "sticks and stones may break my bones, but words will never harm me" resemble this passage?

8. In 2:8-9 and 3:1-3, describe what Ezekiel was told to eat and what it tasted like:

    a. Why do you think it tasted sweet? (Compare with Ps. 19:7-10; 119:97-104)

9. Do you think that Ezekiel 3:3, 10 have anything in common with John 6:35, 53-58? Explain.

10. In Ezekiel 3:5-6, is God sending the prophet to a foreign country so that he would have to learn a new language and learn about their culture to be an effective missionary? Explain.

11. In our day, does God send us anywhere? If He does, where does He send us? (Verses, please)

12. The children of Israel should listen to the prophet, but in Ezekiel 3:7, what does God predict they will do and why?

13. If the word of God told YOU a *thus says the Lord*, what would YOU do?

1   Who Should I Talk To?

Before Ezekiel ever shared God's message, and before he ever preached, taught, or modeled the word of the Lord—God told Ezekiel to eat the word, to take it into his heart, and to listen closely (Ez. 2:9-3:3).

God told Christians, as well, to eat the word, take it into our hearts, to listen closely, and to tell everybody about the word (Jn. 6:48-58; Mt. 11:15; 28:19-20; 2 Tim. 4:2; Heb. 5:12-14). We need a full plate of God's word each and every day (Heb. 5:14). Times will come when we will feel like Ezekiel, "overwhelmed" in our spirit while facing our neighbors with God's word (Ez. 3:15); but sooner or later, we will learn that God means what He says when telling us to inform others about His message. Ezekiel and the other prophets did what God asked, and the apostles, Paul and John, learned to have the boldness to speak God's word, even when threatened by people who wanted to stop them. We will thrive healthily on a steady diet of God's word, which will build strong spirits within us, so we can go confidently to our neighbors and say, "This is what the Lord says." *(Based on a study-thought by P. Alley, in the Wednesday Evening Bible Class, 1996, El Cajon, CA)*

Many Christians, who have the truth of God's word at their disposal, tend to keep it to themselves for a variety of reasons, although the biggest reason, I think, is fear. The fear of losing jobs, losing friends, making waves, and losing family members stay at the top of the Fear List. I, for one, find it difficult talking to people about the Bible, because I become too intense, both physically and verbally; probably like many grandparents do when they start up about their grandchildren, or like sports fanatics when they get on about their favorite team's statistics and players. You almost have to wave your arms and grab my attention to make me stop talking. I'm so into the topic that I don't even know where I am. Since I tend to chase people away with my fervor, I don't share my faith with them. But God says that I, as a Christian, must study His words and share them. He says to do it with love for the ones with whom I am sharing, even if they run away from me when they see me coming. God says that when people dread my coming, it is their problem, not mine.

Several thousand years ago, a priest of God named Ezekiel had to deal with this same problem, when he became a captive in the land of the Babylonians, far from his native Judah. He, and many of his fellow countrymen, were forced to live near the river Chebar. According to *Bible-History.com* (which has information from several well-known Bible dictionaries) the Chebar was most probably a great, royal canal that Nebuchadnezzar built to connect the Tigris and the Euphrates rivers; and the captive Jews were being used as forced-labor (http://www.bible-history.com/links.php.....Chebar). Some Bible versions even say that they lived by the "Chebar canal" as opposed to a "river." Regardless, Ezekiel was a normal, average guy, who had a wife, and who worked alongside all the other prisoners—when one special day, God came for a visit.

On that memorable day, Ezekiel had "the hand of the Lord" placed on him and God's words came to him and changed his life forever. What would it feel like to have "the hand of the Lord" laid upon me? Not only did God's words come to Ezekiel, but mental videos of heavenly places and God's throne room came at him, too. Did Ezekiel think he had gone insane? We don't know, but he did sit or stand there and watch the visions as he looked up to the sky (not unlike Steven when he saw the Lord in Acts 7:55, 56). Ezekiel wrote down what he saw, which closely resembled what the apostle John saw in his book of Revelation, hundreds of years later. At the end of the first chapter in Ezekiel's book, a powerful person started talking to the prisoner-priest; a person who could radiate His own light, His own force-field. The mental videos frightened Ezekiel so much that he fell down onto his face in terror, but the Powerful One ordered him to stand and listen, and even lifted Ezekiel up onto his feet.

At that moment, the Lord officially commissioned Ezekiel as His messenger to the captive Israelites. Ezekiel had to communicate with them what God said—no more, no less—and he had to express to the people God's words even if they did not want to hear, or even if they refused to hear, or even if they became angry and tortured Ezekiel in any way. Interestingly, the Lord made it extremely clear that Ezekiel did not have to go to a foreign nation where they couldn't understand his language. The Israelites in captivity had no excuse for not understanding what God wanted them to know, because they could understand the language that Ezekiel used. Throughout his book, Ezekiel described the various times when God commanded him to act out visual analogies in order to graphically explain God's words, and he told about speaking God's words, teaching the people, telling the people off, and encouraging them to be faithful to God, and to be righteous.

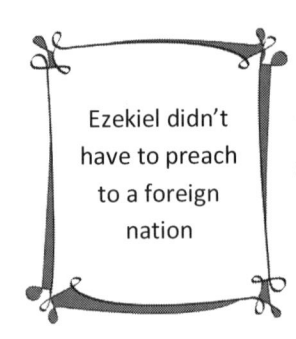

> Ezekiel didn't have to preach to a foreign nation

We can find this same type of commission given to Christians today, in Matthew 28:19, 20. The Lord told His followers to make more students out of all the world's people, by baptizing them with the authority of God, Jesus, and the Holy Spirit, and then teaching those students everything that the Lord taught His followers. The only difference between Ezekiel and us today is that we are to tell what God says to everybody who speaks our own language and also to everybody who speaks foreign languages. We have to tell folks the words of God even if they make fun of us, yell, slam doors, walk away, or even torture us in some way. We do not have to fear what others can do or say, which means that I am not to even fear my own *fervor*, as I mentioned earlier.

We must take a stand, take God's words into our minds, hearts, and our lives, and then go out and share them—no matter if they are rebellious Christians, fallen Christians, or people who have never obeyed the gospel. Ezekiel showed us many ways in which we can share the word of God, not only by teaching and speaking, but also by graphic, living examples. However, before Ezekiel could do this new job, he had to get into God's word and put God's word into himself. God expects no less from us today (Jn. 6:31-68).

Ask these questions of yourself: do I stand in God's presence, do I feed on God's Word, do I allow the Word to digest throughout my thoughts and actions, and do I share the Word?

--Notes--

--Notes--

Truly, truly, I say to you, if anyone keeps My word he shall never see death.
John 8:51

Lesson Two
The Watchman

Fill in the Blanks: Ezekiel 3:27 (Make adjustments depending on your translation version)

"But when _____ with you, I will _____, and you shall say to them, '_____.' He who _____, let him _____; and he who _____, let him _____: for they are a _____."

Questions:

1. Do you think that the God of the Bible keeps people in the dark about how He will judge us? Explain.

2. Name some people in the Bible whom God warned about impending doom if they did not repent.

3. What does Ezekiel 3:18 mean to you in your life?

4. According to verse 19, should we feel guilty if, after warning someone from danger, they choose not to listen?

5. What if the person or persons that we talk to hate us for "meddling" in their lives and how does this compare to how people treated Jesus? (Gal. 4:16; Ezek. 2:6)

6. In Ez. 3:18-21, what exactly are we to warn others from?

7. Further on, in Ez. 33:1-6, what real life picture is painted?

(continued next page)

8. What are some other words or synonyms for *watchman*?

9. What does Ezek. 33:7-9 have in common with Acts 4:18-20 and Mark 16:15-16?

10. Back in Ez. 3:27, what does this verse have in common with Rev. 2:7, 11, and 17, and Matt. 11:15?

Bonus Question:

    Today, this week, this month, is there anybody in your life you can talk to, encourage, reason with, or warn about the Living God? Will you obey God or will you be afraid?

2 The Watchman

In the New Testament, people like the apostle Paul had the job of *planting* the word of God in people's hearts, which means *preaching*. Throughout Paul's letters, he constantly warns Christians of judgment to come when we must face our Maker. He also warns Christians to hunt and search out things, things like behaving sexually pure, and things like behaving righteously, because without these behaviors, we cannot—we will not—see God. Other people, like the evangelist Apollos, had the job of *watering* the Word of God, which means *teaching*. Teaching builds on the preaching already done by someone else (1 Cor. 3:6).

The Lord orders Christians today to also plant or to preach His word into people's hearts. God told us not to *force* people to be dunked in water, or to brainwash, or to please people, but to just preach, teach, baptize, and encourage. Preaching and teaching warns others about a day of judgment when the Lord will come in flaming fire to take everybody to face Him and be assessed for what we have done, said, or thought. Then, based on that assessment, we will be sent to one of two places forever and ever. One place has no light; with an eternal fire for souls to burn in, without the hope of relief, and it has absolutely nothing good to experience, which could even mean not having the company of other sufferers (because company is a good thing, Gen. 2:18). The other place where people can be sent contains lots of light, life, blessings, good friends, singing, happiness, health, rest, no suffering in any way, and just everything that is good, everything that is fresh, and everything that is new.

Like Paul, Noah also preached God's word, spreading the news to people living in his time about the world's approaching watery destruction. He preached by his actions, his behavior, and by words, while he worked on God's vessel of salvation during a period of one hundred years. Only his immediate family members listened to him and believed. The rest of the world made fun of Noah, and then they died in the cataclysmic flood that he had preached about!.

> Whether they obeyed or not, didn't concern Ezekiel

A few thousand years later, God told the priest, Ezekiel, to speak His word, telling the truth to a sinful people called the Israelites. Whether the people obeyed or did not obey, could not concern Ezekiel; he just had orders to preach and to teach. He preached about the reason why they lived as slaves in Babylon: they had turned their backs on God, and they still lived their lives contrary to God's words. More suffering would come if those people did not change their ways and return to living the way God wanted them to live.

In Ezekiel 3:16-17 and Ezekiel 33:1-20, God explained in detail the job of a watchman. A watchman keeps his eyes peeled open at his post to make sure no enemy approaches to cause harm. If a watchman sees any trouble coming, he must sound the alarm, make the warning, shout, tell everyone, explain, give the details, and in other words—do his job. If people ignore him, do not believe him, or just don't care, then when death and suffering overtake them, they have no one to blame but themselves; but God will reward the watchman. On the other hand, if the people listen to the watchman and rearrange their lives so as to protect themselves from approaching danger, they will live, and the watchman will also be well rewarded.

Christians today are God's watchmen. God has told us in His word that an awful day of judgment is coming when no one will be expecting it, and if the people do not arrange their lives so as to protect themselves from the approaching danger, they will die eternally. And if people have not received a warning about it, their blood will be placed on the Christians around them who did not sound the warning! At least that's what I get out of it, and it scares me to the bone. How many souls have passed by me, without my mouth opening in warning of the impending judgment and of the need to live righteous lives (Acts 24:24, 25)? From now on, I'll strive to be brave in helping people protect themselves from the fury of the Living God against the disobedient, those who are ignorant of Him, and also to the evildoers (2 Thess. 1:5-12).

It seems that more and more people today believe in growth and in making churches "grow." The awesome importance of preaching "this is what the Lord God says" does not appear in their religious and spiritual actions. The religious leaders of Ezekiel's day behaved in the same manner. They preached what the people wanted to hear, "peace, peace" even when they were in the lap of captivity, in a foreign land, and forced into slavery (Ez. 13:1-11).

God hasn't changed any since Ezekiel's day and, sad to say, neither have humans.

We must never forget our job in the sight of the living God who watches us. Let us not behave like actors on reality television shows, when it seems like they forget about the cameras trained on them and then they behave like jerks toward each other. We're not on television, but God definitely records what we say and do in a heavenly book, and we will be judged by what we do and what we say.

If we are not *watchmen*, then we need to listen to the other Christians who are brave enough to warn us with God's word, regardless of the traditions and thoughts of other humans. To survive the Day of Judgment, we must arrange our lives so that we are protected from—safe from—eternal doom. This means we believe the words of God, believe in the Word of God (Jesus), wash our sins away in water immersion, stay faithful, and live righteously until we take our last breath (the book of Acts; Rev. 2-3).

--Notes--

--Notes--

He who has an ear, let him hear what the Spirit says...
Rev. 2:7

Lesson Three
The Arrogance

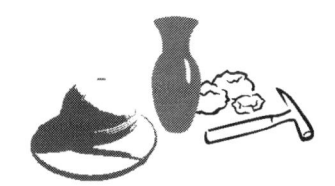

Questions: Ezekiel 5 – 7

- Ez. 5:5 What did God do for Jerusalem?

- Ez. 5:6 What did Jerusalem do to God in return?

- Ez. 5:9, 10 This verse is almost the same as what Daniel said in Daniel 9:11, 12. Daniel lived in Babylon about the same time as Ezekiel at the Chebar. What did these two men say about the disaster their nation was experiencing?

- Ez. 5:11 When God's people in the Old Testament sinned and disobeyed God, what did they actually defile?
    - In relation to this, when Christians sin and disobey God, what do we defile today? (1 Cor. 3:16, 17)

- Ez. 5:11 When is God not a sweet, kind, loving, wonderful being?

    - How does He behave during those times?

- Ez. 7:3 According to what two things did God judge the Jews during Ezekiel's time?

    - According to Jesus Christ, what will God judge us by today? (Matt. 16:27; Rom. 2:6; others?)

- Ez. 7:10 This verse is referring to what Old Testament story? (Num. 16:41-17:12)

(continued next page)

- What does Ezekiel 7:10 and the story about Aaron's rod mean?

- Ez. 7:19 Think of a modern catchy phrase, or a modern proverb, that this verse can be reduced to?

  - Find at least one New Testament passage dealing with money. _____

- Ez. 7:23, 24 Exactly what land is being discussed here?
  - What was this land full of?

BONUS QUESTIONS:

1. In Ezekiel 6:14 and 7:4, 9, 27, during the punishments and destructions and judgments which God dealt out to these people, what were these people **to know**?

2. What does the word *lord* mean?

3. How can the church today become arrogant and what would the outward signs be? (verses?)

3 The Arrogance

According to Ezekiel chapters 6 and 7, the reason behind the nation of Israel turning their backs on God and behaving worse than the wicked nations around them, was because they had become *full of themselves*, or arrogant. They thought more highly of themselves than they ought to, and began making adjustments to God's law and to God's temple. They got to the point that they did not see anything wrong with tacking on to the law of Jehovah God the traditions and religious practices of men from the surrounding nations. This behavior gradually led to terrible human sacrifices (that of children and babies, of course), sexual parties, lusty festivals, bringing in richly decorated statues into God's temple building, astrology, witchcraft, and much more. God put up with it a long time, by continuously sending preachers to the people, to the leaders of the land, and to the leaders of His religion, to make them change their lives and return to being good honest people. The Lord's preachers also told the Israelites that a foreign power would come one day to kill them and take any survivors into slavery, if they did not change their disobedient ways. But, hey, who has ears to hear?

The reason for people choosing not to be good, not to be honest, not to do what God wants them to do, is because of arrogance, pride, egotism, feelings of superiority—in other words, people put their own wants and desires above anything that God wants. People who disregard God's wishes and words do so at great peril, because how can a created being dictate laws to their Creator? It is illogical, nonsensical; like a puppy howling at night because it does not want to sleep where you want it to sleep, or a small child having a tantrum in the store because he wants the super, sugary cereal, while you want his teeth to grow strong.

Even under the Law of Christ, found in the New Testament, God warns His people over and over again not *to think more highly of themselves than they ought* (Rom. 12:3, 16; 11:20; Jas. 4:6, 10; 1 Pet. 5:5, 6), because when we do, we set ourselves up as gods, and we worship what we want to worship in the ways that we want to, while totally ignoring our Creator. What gall. What arrogance.

> When we become arrogant, we become God's enemies

In 1 Peter 5:5-6, God says that He *resists* the proud—the arrogant. *Resist* also means *oppose, refuse to accept, defy, stand against, fight back, combat, go up against, and be against*. Let's think about this a moment. It does not sound all that important when we only read the word *resist*, right? But if we understand that the word *resist* actually means something on the violent side, it can change the whole meaning of the verse. If we read all the different definitions, we'll see that God opposes, hates, is against, and ranges Himself against the proud, rather like a massive army setting itself up against a smaller enemy, and people who are full of self-pride are the enemy!

When we become too arrogant to allow God to make the rules, then we become His enemies. When we are too proud to humble ourselves and behave like God's obedient servants, then we set ourselves up as His boss. Throughout the pages of the Bible, God repeats incessantly that He hates the arrogant (Pro. 8:13; 6:16-19). There is a verse somewhere saying that pride goes before a fall, and there is the story about the rich man and his new barns and how proud he was with himself, but that night God ended his life (Lk. 12:16-21). Also, King Nebuchadnezzar once became full of himself and God forced him to become like a wild beast for a long period of time, until he woke up and voluntarily humbled himself.

That's the key. We all, from the super-rich and intelligent to the lowest, most ignorant human, will be bending our knees and bowing before God Almighty on the Day of Judgment. Every single person since Adam and Eve will either humble ourselves happily (because we're used to it) or miserably (because we're used to having our own way); either way, we will experience humility. The important thing is not waiting too long to learn it. God says that if we voluntarily bend our minds to obey His wishes, then God will exalt us. *Exalt*, what does that mean? It means that God Himself will praise us, applaud us, sing our praises, and magnify us—lifting us up from normalcy to power. Wow. That would so be worth it. On the other hand, if we don't allow God to be the master of our lives, then God himself will resist us, and stand against us, so we cannot enter into His heavenly land, which reminds me of the Cherubim standing at the gate to the Garden of Eden, warding Adam and Eve off from returning, using a fiery sword (Gen. 3:23, 24).

Food for thought, don't you think?

--Notes--

--Notes--

But if you have bitter jealousy and strife in your hearts, do not glory and lie against the truth. James 3:14

Lesson Four

The Idol of Jealousy

Questions:

1. What do you think that the "idol of jealousy" means in Ezekiel 8:3, 5?

2. Read Ezekiel 8:7-12. What do you think verses 7 and 8 mean in connection with verse 12?

3. In verse 14 who or what were the women weeping for and who or what was it? (Google it)

4. In verse 16, what were the men worshipping and exactly where were they worshipping?

5. Explain how passages like Rom. 12:2; Gal. 1:6-10 relate to the problem of worshiping like the "nations" around us?

6. In Ezekiel 9:4, what kind of people does God mark for safe keeping? (Is. 33:14-16)

    a. What happens to those who do not have the mark of God's safekeeping?

    b. Explain any similarities this has with the 10th plague in Egypt.

7. In Ezekiel 9:6, where does this judgment, this killing start? _____

8. In the New Testament, what does Peter tell us where the Judgment will begin? (look in 1 Peter 4:17)

(continued next page)

9. Read Ezekiel 11:5-12. According to verse 12, is it all right to act according to the standards and laws of the nations around us when it concerns worshipping God? Why or why not?

10. What are some of the descriptions of the church today in 1 Peter 2:9-11?

11. Portions of the passage in 1 Peter 2:6-11 are quotes from the Old Testament; what are God's feelings towards the church in comparison to His people under His Old Law, in Ezekiel's day?

　　a. How jealous do you think God gets for His people today? Any other verses?

Bonus Questions:

A. What leader in the Old Testament thought he could change God's law to fit his needs by making himself a priest and prophet, and what caused him to do this deed, and what did God do to him? (2 Chr. 26:14-21)

B. Did any of the people listed in this lesson's scriptures in Ezekiel get away with hiding from God? Why, or why not? (Heb. 4:12, 13)

C. What famous Old Testament prophet tried to run away and hide from God? Did he succeed or not, and why?

4. The Idol of Jealousy

Roving eyes kept cropping up throughout the history of the Israelites. They constantly had the deep desire to acquire the trash that other nations had, while letting go of the magnificent treasure that God had already freely given them.

- The Israelites begged Moses to let them return to slavery, because they wanted leeks and onions instead of freedom (Num. 11:4-6).
- Then the Israelites wanted an earthly king like the nations around them, instead of Jehovah God (1 Sam. 8:4-7).
- Many times, the Israelites embraced the power, control, and sensual pleasures that the idols of the nations provided (Judges—2 Chronicles).

The people of God were eaten up with jealousy. Jealousy became the biggest idol the Jews ever worshipped. Ezekiel saw it sitting in the entry way of the Temple of Jehovah God. Yes, they may have had some kind of physical statue there, of a heathen god, but the Lord specifically called it *Jealousy*. Whether it was God's jealousy for His people or the people's envy of worldly pleasures, it did not matter, it still ended up with the people's destruction.

The Jews collected gods like people today collect stamps, coins, cars or DVD's. They found it impossible to only have their own unique God, of whom others might copy. They wanted what everyone else had. They didn't want to be different. Set apart. Exceptional. Free.

Many of our brethren in God's church today have the same roving eyes. Jealousy, envy, greed, and pride lead them to behave like the Jews in Ezekiel's time—hiding behind the walls of the Temple of the Living God, while worshiping and fondling all the idols (manmade activities or fame) that they have found in the world. Like the Jews, our brethren want to use the church that Christ built as a front, a cover, while they behave like the *nations* around them, observing human religious traditions and myths that have nothing to do with God's word or with truth. They do not display enough honesty to walk away from the Lord's church, in order to join the denominations or world religions. They remain in the church that Christ started and then entice or coerce other members into falling away with them from the truth, so they can follow human teachings and rules. They don't want to be different. Set apart. Unique. Free.

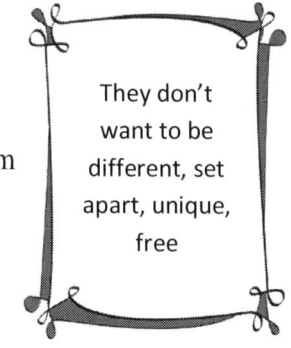

> They don't want to be different, set apart, unique, free

The Lord told Ezekiel and the other prophets that He destroyed the nation of Israel, sending the survivors off into slavery, due to their *whoring*, which means they behaved like the disobedient nations surrounding them, prostituting themselves with other religions. Even though the religious leaders of Ezekiel's day did some of their *whoring* with the manmade gods in the lower rooms of the Temple, hiding from the general populace, God knew everything they did, and it absolutely nauseated him. It repulsed him. The term w*hore* turns out to be a very offensive name for a prostitute, not only as a noun, but also as a verb. It generally means that someone is extremely sexually active with anybody, or it stands for someone who gives his or her body to others sexually for money. Another meaning for *whore* can be for a person who has no problem disregarding his or her principles or integrity in order to obtain something, usually for selfish reasons. Any of the meanings are the same—self-gratification or selling one's self for money, fame, or lust fulfillment.

When God's people disregard the good principles of their Lord, or when we disregard the integrity that God requires of us, and we lust after what the world has to offer, taking part in what other religions offer, sacrificing truth in order to believe in myths or falsehoods, then God calls that *whoring*. We prostitute ourselves, we become whores (God's choice of words, not mine). We become whores when say we follow Christ, while at the same time we do not live in obedience to God's word. The only reason why this *whore principle* would be hard to understand, would be because a person does not want to humble himself or herself enough to stop sinning, and stop ignoring God's word.

The Lord plainly tells mankind that when He sends judgment on the world, it will begin in the church. He will separate the righteous from the wicked, the sheep from the goats, the weeds from the grain, starting within the church itself (Matt. 13:24-30; 25:32-36; 1 Pet. 4:17, 18). That means the Christians who practice sin in the church, who think they are clever by hiding their dishonesty, or their adoption of other religious practices, will become chaff, or burnable material—weeds. As the church of our Lord and Savior, Jesus Christ, we must make sure that an idol of jealousy does not sit in the entry way of our buildings, our bodies, our minds, or of our hearts.

> "It was for freedom that Christ set us free; therefore keep standing firm
> and do not be subject again to a yoke of slavery." (Gal. 5:1)

--Notes--

--Notes--

He who has an ear, let him hear what the Spirit says...
Rev. 2:7

Lesson Five

Prophet or Profit?

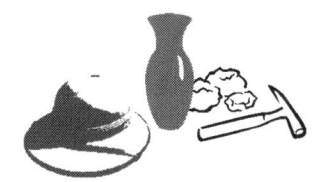

Questions: Ezekiel 13

1. Ez. 13: 2 What did name did God call Ezekiel in this verse? _____

    a. Who in the New Testament was also called this name? _____

    b. Who was Ezekiel to prophesy against?

2. To what group of people within the church today can you compare the job of *prophet*?

3. What were the prophets of Israel doing in verses 2 -7?

    a. Vs. 2 _____
    b. Vs. 3 _____
    c. Vs. 6 _____

4. There are many passages in the New Testament that also deal with false, lying prophets; like 2 Pet. 2:1; Matt. 7:15-21; and 1 John 4:1; Rev. 2:2. What does this tell you about God in our day?

5. In verses 10-16, what exactly do false prophets do when they lie to the people about God's word?

6. In verses 17-23, who else were included with the false prophets in Israel, and what were they doing?

7. Ezekiel is preaching to Judeans, but in the northern kingdom years before, what evil queen did exactly what verses 17-23 discuss *and* what exactly did happen to her (1 Kings 16-21; 2 Kings 9)?

8. In Ezekiel 13:19c, why were all these false prophets so successful in the Old Testament?

9. According to 2 Tim. 4:3-4, why would false prophets, preachers, teachers be successful today?

(continued next page)

10. In Ezekiel 13:20-21, describe the picture God paints depicting what false prophets and diviners (witches) actually do to people.

11. In Ezekiel 13:23, what will God do for the good people?

Bonus Question:
   In reading Matthew 23:1-36, what do you think is the root that produces false preachers, teachers, and leaders?

5   Profit or Prophet?

What could possibly make someone resolve to lie to people about spiritual matters, leading large groups of souls into life-paths that are totally or even partially alien to God's word? The answer can be found in the scriptures.

During ancient times, the true prophets of Jehovah God repeatedly claimed that Judah's leaders judged for a bribe, that her priests instructed for a price, and that the prophets divined for money (Isaiah 1:23; Micah 3:11). All the nation's leaders were greedy for gain, from the kings at the top, all the way down to the prophets. Since the time of Christ, the apostle Peter told us that false prophets and teachers will always operate among people. Someone will always secretly introduce destructive teachings, including denying the divinity of Jesus. Peter said that because of their greed, they will modify the truth and exploit people with deceitful words (2 Pet. 2:1-3). Paul said that these false teachers love only their own selves, money, and pleasure—while they put on a good show of having a form of godliness (Acts 20:29-30; 1 Cor. 11:11-15). They have motives based on making money at the expense of others, or on having power over people, no matter what it takes. Greed proves itself to be the reason for false teachers, both past and present.

The burden of sin doesn't rest only on the shoulders of the lying preachers and teachers, though. These teachers or prophets experience success for the same reason that a good store owner has success —the public wants what they have to offer. Paul wrote that times will come when God's people will not want truthful teaching. People who claim to follow Jesus Christ will find the truth uninteresting, boring, or not pertinent, and they will collect teachers who tell them what they want to hear (2 Tim. 4:3-4).

> Each person has the responsibility of not straying from God's truth

Throughout Ezekiel's book in the Old Testament, he said that he lived in a rebellious house with people who had eyes but would not see and ears that would not hear. That must be why later, the apostle John told his listeners to test the spirits around them, to see if they truly came from God (1 Jn. 4:1), and Paul said Christians need to correctly read and study the Bible (2 Tim. 2:15). In Acts 17:10-13, Paul ran into a group of people who refused to just accept what the great apostle personally taught them. They checked out his teachings by reading through God's words to see if Paul really came from God. Paul proudly called them *noble*. They put effort into their salvation, with fear and trembling (Phil. 2:12). Most people, like those on Mars Hill in Athens, listen to everything, and adopt whatever sounds good or whatever makes them feel good regardless of truth (Acts 17). The truth is, each person bears the responsibility of knowing God's word and not straying from it. If we know the words of God, then uneducated or unscrupulous people cannot get away with deceiving us into wandering away from His truth.

In the words of Jesus Christ, concerning the religious people of His day, "Every plant which my heavenly Father did not plant shall be rooted up. Let them alone, they are blind guides of the blind. And if a blind man guides a blind man, both will fall into a pit," (Matt. 15:13-14).

We must beware of throwing away truths to buy lies—in religion, in politics, and in everyday living. Secular history itself teaches us the horrible danger of this practice, in both personal and national life. Every single time, without fail, when people follow others who flatter them with lies, they eventually fall into destruction. The Israelites of Ezekiel's day had followed speakers and leaders who told them the lies that made them feel good, even while they lived in Babylon as prisoners and slaves! I find it amazing the length people will go to in order to hide from the fact that they live in a toilet bowl, enslaved to sin, and far away from where God wants them to be. Even the prodigal son, in Luke 15, woke up to the truth of his miserable condition in the pig pen, and made the necessary changes to become right with himself and with his father.

What about you?

--Notes--

--Notes--

Test yourselves to see if you are in the faith; examine yourselves!
1 Cor. 13:5-6

Lesson Six

Shepherds and Wolves

Multiple Choice: Ezekiel 14-15; 34:1-10 (Circle **any** answer that applies)

1. Who approached Ezekiel in chapter 14:1?

    a. The men of Israel
    b. The Babylonians
    c. The elders of Israel

2. What question did God put to them in verse 3?

    a. What are your names?
    b. What great things have you done for My people?
    c. Should I be consulted by you?

3. Why would God ask such an insulting question?

    a. Because God was not their only object of worship.
    b. Because the elders were holding onto only a form of godliness, but in their hearts they were not interested in obeying God.
    c. Because they were double-minded and hypocritical.

4. In verses 7-8, what was God going to do to an elder who would not obey Him, while hanging onto the office of eldership?

    a. God would set His face against that man and cut him off from the people.
    b. God would make him a sign and a proverb.
    c. God would deal with him personally.

5. Straying from God by being double-minded, hypocritical, and unfaithful makes us like:

    a. A vine that won't bear fruit. Ez. 15:1-8
    b. A tree that won't bear fruit. Luke 13:6-9
    c. Strong Christians. 3 John 6:2

6. Anything that doesn't do what it is supposed to do is:

    a. Given or sold to someone else who can use it. 1 Tim. 1:19, 20
    b. Destroyed or thrown into the dump. 2 Thess. 1:8-9
    c. Kept anyway for its intrinsic value. 1 Pet. 8:3

Questions:

1. Read Ez. 14:10-11 and explain what God really wants, in verse 11.

(continued next page)

2. Please explain any significance for God to mention Noah, Daniel, and Job in verses 12-20.

3. In chapter 34:1-10, what is another name for elders? _____

4. Exactly who or what does the flock represent? _____

5. List what the elders, or _____, were doing or not doing to the flock:

6. To whom does the flock belong, according to verse 6? _____

7. To whom do the shepherds belong, according to verse 8? _____

8. In verse 10, what will God demand from the wicked shepherds, and why?

9. Please tell what you think about the following New Testament passages and what they have to do with this lesson: Titus 1:7-16; Acts 20:28-35; 1 Peter 5:1-4; Matt. 20:25-28; Rom. 16:17-18

10. If the God of the New Testament is the same God of the Old Testament, then what should that mean to those who are leaders in the church today?

6 Shepherds and Wolves

One fine day, Ezekiel sat down somewhere, perhaps in front of his house. Apparently, he was minding his own business, or chatting with friends, when a group of Israelite leaders approached to seek God's advice, or prophecies, from this priest. God immediately, and angrily, told Ezekiel to tell them His message. The very first thing God asked the leaders was an apparently offensive question, "…these men have taken their false gods into their hearts and put before their faces the sin which is the cause of their fall: am I to give ear when they come to me for directions?" (Ez. 14:3 BBE) The English Standard Version says, "…Should I indeed let myself be consulted by them?" God boldly says that their sinful deeds meant that God would not even consider listening to their requests or comments (Is. 59:1,2).

What an extraordinary thing, to have an eternal being, an all-powerful, all-knowing, and an all-everywhere being, suddenly ask you a question. Any question, any comment, from such a being would be an honor for most people, but to have an insulting question like the one God asked on that particular day should logically cause anxiety for those being asked—if they really thought about it. When an all-mighty being says something like: "You are filthy, dirty, and stink like a skunk! How dare you approach Me, your Royal King, your Creator?" I think I'd probably be looking for a rock to hide under!

In the church, just because a person is a leader, a preacher, a teacher, an elder, or a deacon does not mean that they are worth following or listening to, and God will sooner or later point out that fact, usually in front of witnesses (how embarrassing). Most of the leaders and prophets, in Ezekiel's day, still worked and practiced, even in captivity, but they did not worship God the way He had prescribed to Moses. They instead worshiped the idols of Canaan and listened to astrologers and magicians, as substitutes for God's word in order to find out how to live. Some of them hid the fact that they believed in foreign gods, but God knows everything, and nothing can be hidden from Him (Heb. 4:12, 13).

People who aspire to be leaders in God's church, must be very aware that God holds them responsible for following His will, His words, His law. Leaders and preachers who take people farther and farther away from God's word and law, by telling them things that make them feel good and feel accepted, will eventually receive a terrible punishment. The Israelite prophets told God's people that peace was just around the corner and that everything was all right. Isaiah, years before, said that the leaders and prophets liked to lead God's people

> The people of God are God's, not the human leaders'

astray, to be swallowed up by terrible things, and God would not have mercy on the young, the old, the orphans, or even the widows, because they all willingly followed those sinful authority figures (Is. 9:14-21). The influential did not listen to Isaiah's warnings, which occurred long before Babylon struck, instead they continued to gradually move farther and farther away from God's law, all for their own gain.

Ezekiel told the leaders that the people they led belonged to God (Ez. 34:1-10). What a concept for them to hear. Most leaders, even today, especially in religion, feel that people who follow them, belong to them. What? Did they create those people, cause them to exist? God said that the Israelites were His own personal flock, His sheep, and the leaders and prophets were His shepherds who, instead of leading the flock to good pastures and water, were slaughtering the sheep, even eating them, and leaving the rest to starve or be eaten by wild beasts. This reminds me of when Peter said that Satan himself runs around like a roaring lion, searching to devour any unlucky game. The Israelite shepherds, in Judah and in Babylon, had the habit of letting Satan come into the pen that held God's sheep, whenever Satan wanted fresh meat!

In the New Testament, the leaders of God's flock, including preachers and teachers, are also told how to behave (1 Tim. 3; Tit. 1; 2 Tim. 4:1-5). But in 2 Timothy 4:1-5, Paul warned Timothy (a preacher) that the flock would try and stray off to follow myths, or other teachings, and would look for shepherds that would deliver falsehood to them! It's not always the shepherds' fault for sheep going astray. As a sheep, are you going off on your own, behind your good leaders' backs and getting lost all the time? As a follower, are your leaders on the right track? Are you following along without checking the map, the Bible? If you are following the wrong leaders, or leader, you cannot blame them in the end, because God has also given you His words to guide you in the right way. Hey, just saying.

--Notes--

--Notes--

Discovering Ezekiel

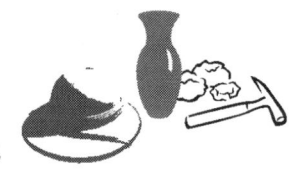

Come here, I shall show you the bride, the wife of the Lamb.
Rev. 21:9

Lesson Seven

This Groom Is a Special Kind of Lover

Questions:

1. Describe the picture that Ezekiel 16:1-5 paints.

2. In verse 6, what did God see in the open field when He was passing by, and who does it represent?

   a. Did God really have to do anything for Israel? _____

   b. What parallels can you find between this passage and Jesus' parable of the Good Samaritan in Luke 10:29-37?

3. What did God "say" in verse 6, and why do you think He repeated himself?

4. In verse 7, what did God do for Israel when she was helpless?

5. In Ez. 16:8, what does it mean when God says Israel became His? _____

6. In Ez. 16:8-14, list the things that God personally did for Israel:

7. In verse 14, when the Israelites were at their peak of perfection, whose splendor were they actually showing off?

8. At what point do you think the Israelites were actually at the peak of splendor as a nation? Explain.

(continued next page)

39

9. Please tell how Ezekiel 16:1-14 parallels the history of the church in the New Testament.

10. What New Testament passages teach us that the church is the bride of Christ? (Google it)

11. Do you think that God's bride (Israel) in the Old Testament had any say in religious matters? Explain.

12. Do you believe that the church today has any say in the matters of how to worship God, or how to be saved, or how to act as Christians? Explain.

13. How do you think that the church today can show off the splendor of her husband (Jesus)?

14. What can you personally do to help display the riches and splendors of God to those around you?

15. Did the Israelites deserve God's love? _____
16. Did they deserve to be married to the Living God? _____
17. Are Christians any different than the Israelites? _____
18. What does Romans 5:5-11 and Ephesians 5:25-27 tell you about the awesome love of God?

7 — Here Comes the Bride!

As my wedding day approached, everyone clearly informed me that the whole day was *my* day. I was the reigning queen and my wish was their command. They proved it by taking care of everything dealing with the wedding. I chose my invitations and theme, but the others did the rest. People were all over the place, and nobody left me alone. In fact, I would dream in the middle of the night that crowds of people stared at me while I slept. Several times, I had to turn on the light to chase them out of my room. Of course, I was just dreaming, but it sure felt real.

The church is the bride, today. The bride of Christ. As family members of the bride, we must realize that she is the reigning queen and her wish is our command. We need to make sure that she is beautiful and ready for her groom. We must leave nothing undone because a wedding is a precious thing. We must never leave her alone, tirelessly taking care of all her needs. We strive to impress the bride and the groom with the results. When a wedding goes perfectly, it creates a great feeling inside of everybody. We can look back at the photos and videos and feel a sense of pride, a sense of teamwork, a sense of accomplishment.

How do you feel about the bride of Christ? Are you excited about the wedding? Are you excited about your part in the preparations?

This Groom is a Special Kind of Lover

Just picture in your mind a man walking through his fields and stumbling across the horrible sight of a newly born baby girl, uncleaned, unwanted, uncared for, writhing in her birthing blood, and crying pathetically; abandoned and alone—left to die. Like the blood of Abel crying from the ground after Cain murdered him, so this infant cries from the ground, drenched in her blood. The man takes immediate compassion on the little dying life-form, calling the ambulance and the police, and when they cannot find the real mother, he takes care of the baby until she is grown. He pays for her education, rich clothing, the best of jewelry, the best of care and protection, and he is so proud of her. Eventually, he asks her to marry him and she accepts his hand in marriage. Everybody adores her because of her beauty and all the wealth that her husband lavishes on her. This husband, this groom, is a special kind of lover.

The man loved the baby even when she was dying, weak, and helplessly groveling in blood; when the baby had no idea of who her new protector was and could not even say thank you. He loved the little girl by giving her what she needed to grow up and take care of herself. He loved the young woman by continuing to care for her and give her all she needed to appear gloriously beautiful. This husband spared no expense for the little orphan, at a time in history when baby girls were not generally wanted, and their deaths did not mean anything to people. This groom had willed the baby to live, making sure that she could live.

This husband, groom, man—is God Almighty. He just loves taking nothing and turning it into something magnificent. He hates seeing abuse that people inflict on one another, even to women. God provides help in times of trouble (Ps. 46:1).

The people, called Israel, in the Old Testament, started their existence when God and one lonely old man, named Abraham, and his old wife, named Sarah, wandered around the fields and deserts of Canaan; living in a tent. From such an inauspicious beginning, sprang a nation that later ruled over that same land. Under the reigns of David and Solomon, Israel became like a shining light among the nations. People even traveled from faraway places to see the glory of Israel and the great things in which the nation took part. Israel won all their battles, conquered peoples, showed mercy, and everything turned to gold at their touch. God caused all this to happen, and we can read about it from Genesis through the book of 1 Kings.

The people, called the Church in the New Testament, have the same kind of history. We can read about it from the book of Acts to Revelation. The Church started her existence with God and one man named Jesus, with His twelve students. Those thirteen men wandered all over the modern land of Canaan, called Judea by that time, without a place to call their own. When Jesus was crucified, His blood splattered all over the Jewish courts, the Roman courts, and the courts of the Edomites (Herod), and the hilltop outside the boundaries of those courts. When God sees people "wallowing" in the blood of Christ (through baptism—Romans 6), He wills them to "Live!" The Church lived and grew to be a mighty and a holy nation of priests, even until today. She scattered over the whole earth, making more and more people, called the Church. The Church is the bride of Jesus, who is the son of God, and Jesus right now lavishes riches upon her beyond measure (Eph. 5:22-33; Rev. 19:7-9), like forgiveness of wrongs, freedom from living in evil, freedom to do good, the freedom to be clean and clothed in righteousness, and having the expectations of getting to live with Jesus in immeasurably rich mansions in heaven, forever. The Church should be a shining light among the nations—doing good deeds to all people, teaching people about Jesus and Heaven, and generally being fun to hang around with.

> When God sees people "wallowing" in the blood of Christ...

What is so special about God, is that He shows no partiality. He could marry "blue-bloods" or royalty, but instead He chooses to marry the impoverished, the injured, the abandoned, the hated, and the helpless. He is kind, compassionate, protective, concerned, and interested in our growth. He loves to see us clothed in His wealth of blessings. He sacrifices everything for our good and well-being. God was the perfect husband in the Old Testament and His son is the perfect husband in the New Testament, and His gorgeous eyes are fixed upon His bride, and Jesus just oozes affection for her.

God calls every living human to be one of the people called the Church, His son's bride. We can accept His invitation and let God cleanse us and fix us up into the best-of-the-best kind of people, or we can reject His call and wander around the dusty fields and deserts of life, without any purpose or protection. Which would you rather be, a newborn, uncared for, unloved, or a newborn lavished with wealth and love?

--Notes--

--Notes--

Humble yourself in the sight of the Lord and he will exalt you.
James 4:10

Lesson Eight

How to Be Twice as Bad as Sodom and Gomorrah

Questions: Ezekiel 16:15-59

1. With what sort of things do people have a tendency to place their trust?

2. In Ezekiel 16:15, what does God call the action of placing our trust anywhere else but in Him?

3. In reading verses 16-21, compare them with Deuteronomy 6:10-12 and explain your comparison.

4. Read Ezekiel 16: 14-22, and compare them with Revelation 2:4-5, explaining **how** Christians can fall from God's grace as the Israelites did.

5. Please list the things which God said belonged to Him in verses 14-22:
    a.   e.
    b.   f.
    c.
    d.

6. Do you think that this list includes everything from necessities to luxuries? Explain.

7. In reading Ezekiel 16:23-34, what was "the difference" between the prostitution (or apostasy) of God's people and regular prostitutes?

8. In verse 32, we find another term besides prostitute for the people of God who are falling away. What is it?

9. In the Mosaic Law, what was the judgment against a couple committing adultery? (Lev. 20:10).

(continued next page)

10. What is the common denominator in verses 22 and 43?

11. In verse 49, God lists the reasons for the wickedness of Sodom and Gomorrah; what were they?

    a.

    b.

    c.

12. In verses 49-50, what did these three reasons result in?

    a.

    b.

    c.

13. What did God do to them when He saw these things? _____

14. In verse 51, just how sinful were the Judeans?

15. When we break our covenant with God, what exactly are we doing, according to verse 59?

16. In reading the passage for this lesson, and 1 Peter 4:17-18, will God judge the church (His people) differently from the world? Explain your answer.

8   How to Be Twice as Bad as Sodom and Gomorrah

Just as all things have a beginning, all things will have an ending; and in the end, a judgment will come, on all people, past and present. "A judgment?" you ask. "What ever happened to a trial and a fair hearing?" There won't be a trial on that last day, because the trial is taking place right now, while we live and breathe. Heavenly lawyers are gathering all the trial evidence in each person's case and are assessing the evidence at this very moment—every thought, intention, action, and word, is being recorded—and when we take our last breath, the trial will have finished. Then, the Judge will pass judgment on each person. This Judge just happens to be the one who caused everything to begin, way back in the beginning, and He's the one who forms each of us in the womb. Since He knows everything about us, every hair on our head or lack thereof, our personal history, our thoughts, and everything else about us, He ought to be able to come to a fair and unprejudiced judgment, especially after going over our life-evidence (Heb. 9:27; 10:26-31, 39).

"What will He judge us on," you ask? He gave us a manual to read and live by, called the Bible, so we can receive a reward at the end of all days, if we want; but He also gave us the freedom to disregard the manual, the map, the instructions, if we so desire; and hang it all, if there aren't a whole lot of people who just hate to use instructions or maps or manuals, and who prefer to wander around lost before admitting they need help. Sound familiar? But the Judge knew this about people, so He gave us a way to be acceptable to Him, if we can actually break down and admit that we aren't the know-it-alls that we like to think we are.

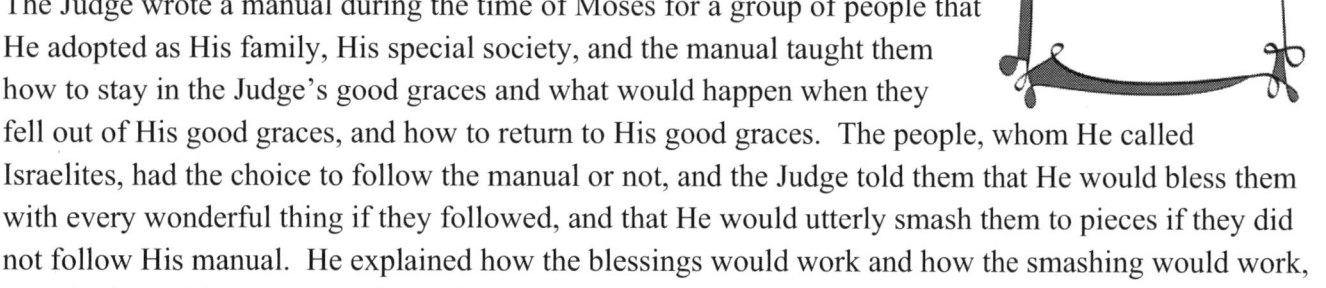

> The judgment happens at the end, while the trial happens as we live on earth

The book of Ezekiel shows us that the Judeans of his day served as prime examples of this freedom of choice and how the Judge does His job. The Judge wrote a manual during the time of Moses for a group of people that He adopted as His family, His special society, and the manual taught them how to stay in the Judge's good graces and what would happen when they fell out of His good graces, and how to return to His good graces. The people, whom He called Israelites, had the choice to follow the manual or not, and the Judge told them that He would bless them with every wonderful thing if they followed, and that He would utterly smash them to pieces if they did not follow His manual. He explained how the blessings would work and how the smashing would work, so nobody could ever say, "Why is this happening to me?"

The thing is, at the time of Ezekiel, the Judge had already begun to smash His society to pieces, using Nebuchadnezzar of Babylon, and He was getting ready to smash again, one last final blow that would pretty much annihilate Judea and Jerusalem, the capital of the society that was supposed to be the Judge's people. The people, even working as slaves in Babylon, still thought everything was okay and that their Lord was still a loving, kind, gracious, peaceful being who would rescue them without the people having to make any changes in their lives. "Changes," you ask? Well, Ezekiel had to tell the people that they had become twice as bad as Sodom and Gomorrah! How can you become twice as bad as Sodom and Gomorrah?

You start out by allowing God to save you from sure death (from the Egyptians or from Satan); and you enjoy tasting and having God's luxuries, protection, and power (a strong kingdom like Solomon's or the blessings of Christ); and then you grow tired of God and start bribing other religions (gods) into your bedchamber (finding everything else in the world much more interesting than God); and you despise the oath you made to God when you took the clean, white clothes that He gave you in baptism (the waters of purification from a gross, bloody condition outside of Christ, Gal. 3:27). The reason why you would be twice as bad as the horrible citizens of Sodom and Gomorrah, would be because those citizens had never made an oath to God, they had never had a pact or agreement with God, they had never lived in God's luxuries, protection, or power, so they could claim ignorance as the reason for their gruesome lifestyles. God still wiped them off the face of the earth, leaving behind only barren ground and salt, but the Israelites, the Judeans, and those who have been saved by Christ, are different. Think "dog/vomit" and "hog/mud," as you visualize the following scene:

You're stuck upside down in a car, painfully hanging from the seat belt, bleeding to death from several deep gashes, broken bones in several places, excruciating pain flooding every one of your senses, and then mercifully, someone runs up and pulls you out of the car, stops the bleeding, puts a covering over you to stop the oncoming shock, calls 911, and then graciously pays your way into and out of the hospital. Later, healed enough to go home, you leave the hospital, after yelling at everyone, sneering at the one who saved you, and you hobble away as if nothing had ever happened, and as if you owed no one for the life you still have. That's called ingratitude, rudeness, crudeness, slimy insensitivity, self-centered jerkiness, and being twice as bad as Sodom and Gomorrah.

> Don't be people who can't remember who they are

When we forget what we were before we met God, before he rescued us from helplessness, from being lost, and from the clutches of sin, and we begin to think we are so wonderful now, because of our own abilities, our own goofy sense of self-worth, and then we "move on" to what we think are bigger and better things, outgrowing the one who made us so wonderful, then we have purposefully become churlish, ungrateful Alzheimer's victims. You say, "Alzheimer's?" Yes, people who can't remember who they are, where they are from, who's taking care of them, or who they belong to. The difference between real Alzheimer's victims and God's people, who turn their backs on God, is that Alzheimer patients can't medically, physically, or scientifically help themselves. It's not their fault. They are innocent of their memory loss. Christians who turn from God to wallow in worldly pleasures, lusts, and passions are not innocent victims; they are dogs that vomit and then turn back around to eat the muck they just threw up; they are hogs that get cleaned up and sanitized, and then make a run for the wettest, smelliest mud hole they can find (2 Pet. 2:20-22).

This is how God's people can become twice as bad as Sodom and Gomorrah. But, thanks be to the Judge, Jesus Christ, as long as we have breath in our bodies, He calls for us to return to sanity and selflessness, kindness and righteousness, eating real food instead of vomit, and staying clean and sanitary instead of living filthy, muddy lives. We can repent (or change) our lives and ask the Judge for leniency and forgiveness; and, bless His heart, the Judge bends over backwards to grant us our heartfelt wishes. He told Ezekiel and the Jews over and over that He does not find any pleasure in the death of lost souls, but that He will not tolerate lost, unrepentant souls in His presence, since they are too stinky—singed with the fires of Hell licking at their coat-tails. If you're in this condition, please be willing to admit it and repent, be washed, be cleansed, and stay in the good graces of the eternal Judge (Jas. 4:10; 1 Cor. 6:9-11).

--Notes--

For I have no pleasure in the death of anyone who dies," declares the Lord God. Ez. 18:32

Lesson Nine

Is Sin Inherited?

Questions: Ezekiel 18

1. Read verse 4. Who owns your soul? _____ Who owns every soul? _____

    a. If any soul sins, what will happen to that soul?

2. Read verses 5-9. What kind of person is this passage discussing? _____
    List the **un**righteous things that this person is **NOT** doing:

    a.

    b.

    c.

    d.

    e.

    f.

3. List the **righteous** things this person **IS** doing:

    a.

    b.

    c.

    d.

    e.

    f.

    g.

4. Because the person in verses 5-9 practices right actions, what declaration does God make about him in verse 9?

5. Read Ezekiel 18: 10. What kind of person do you think God is talking about in this passage?
    _____ List the **un**righteous things this person **IS** doing in verses 10-13:

    a.   h.

    b.   i.

    c.   j.

    d.

    e.

    f.

    g.

(continued next page)

Discovering Ezekiel

6. This second, second person had what kind of father (verse 10)? _____

7. In the second half of verse 13, what four declarations does God make about this second person?

   a.

   b.

   c.

   d.

8. Read Ezekiel 18:14. An evil man fathers a son, but what does the son see in his father's life, and what does he think about it?

   a. In verses 14-17, the son of the evil man chooses to live what kind of life?

9. Read Ezekiel 18:17. Because of this son's righteous life, what will God spare him from, and what gift will God give him in the end?

10. Read Ezekiel 18:18. What will happen to this son's wicked father, and why?

11. Read Ezekiel 18:19. What question would mankind ask God about this scenario?

    a. What logical, repeating argument does God use in answer to mankind's question (vs. 4, 19-22, 24-28)?

12. In verses 23 and 32, what does God find NO pleasure in?

13. What does God tell His people to do in verses 30 and 31, and the end of verse 32?

14. Read Matthew 4:17; 11:20-24; Acts 2:38 and explain any comparisons you find with question 13.

15. Quote at least one (1) verse from the New Testament which deals with each of us having to stand before God only for our own actions.

16. How can Hebrews 13:8 and James 1:17 give you confidence concerning our God?

9 Is Sin Inherited?

"You're trying my patience!" growled the exasperated mother at her little boy in the grocery store.

Trying someone's patience. We do it as children to our parents, and then to our teachers, and then our bosses, spouses, and the laws of the land. We seem to like testing boundaries, and if the boundaries weaken, then we can broaden them to get more of what we think we want. But when we decide to try our God's patience, we actually act frivolous with His kindness and take advantage of His mercy (Rom. 2:4-8). Testing the boundaries that God set up, displays a person's stubborn, unrepentant, and selfishly ambitious heart.

One of the definitions of *patience* is *"capable of calmly awaiting an outcome or a result, not hasty or impulsive."* The apostle Peter teaches that God is not slow, or forgetful, about destroying the universe at the end of time, as people like to think, but instead He's extremely patient (2 Pet. 3:9). God does not want anyone to have to spend eternity in a horrible place called Hell, so God will not haphazardly, or hastily, send people into an outer darkness to burn in an unseen fire. He wants every single soul to repent or change, and do what is right; but sooner or later, God will reach the end of His patience with those of us who refuse to behave rightly.

One of the most beautiful passages in the Bible can be found in Ezekiel chapter eighteen. Ezekiel repeatedly affirms that we have a loving, kind, and patient God. We can place complete confidence in the magnificent justice of our Creator. Our God allows each person to make the decision whether to obey Him or to disregard Him. We each stand on our own decision, not on those of any other person. This is freedom indeed: not inheriting sin. The only factors related to sin that we can *inherit* are the after-effects, or the collateral damage, of someone else's bad choices.

God spends time with the prophet Ezekiel, dissecting the arrangement of how and why He works with people, beginning with the foundational reason: "Behold, all souls are mine...the soul that sins, dies (vs. 4)." As it turns out, absolutely every soul born into this world belongs to God. We do not exist without God's permission, nor do we form in the womb and come forth without His go-ahead.

> Each of us stands before Almighty God because of our own decisions

In Genesis 30:1-2, Jacob's wife, Rachel, could not have children, and she envied her sister, who enjoyed several children. One day, Rachel became fed up with the situation and screamed at Jacob to give her a child, but Jacob defended himself by asking her a very profound question, "Am I in the place of God, who has withheld from you the fruit of the womb?" Many stories about barren women exist in the Bible, because it seems like God wants people to understand that we have no control over the formation of a soul, or the bringing of it into the world; only God has that control (1 Sam. 1; Gen. 25:21; Luke 1). You and I belong to God, whether we like it or not. In Acts 17:24-28, Paul states that God gives every person "life and breath and everything," and also that in God "we live and move and have our very being." Later in his life, Paul has to remind Christians that we are not our own, because Jesus bought us with the price of His life's blood, meaning that we must respect God and His wishes with our very bodies, not just with our words or feelings (1 Cor. 6:19-20).

Therefore, since we are God's personal possessions, (an alien thought for Americans), then we really ought to take the time to learn about and understand God's house rules. After giving Ezekiel the foundation for why we should listen to him, God spent the rest of chapter eighteen, using eight-hundred-some-odd words to explain His rules, in detail, on how we should behave; that is, how everybody should behave who live and breathe the air that the Lord created, using the lungs that He also provided.

>"'Cast away from you all your transgressions which you have committed, and make yourselves a new heart and a new spirit! For why will you die…? For I have no pleasure in the death of anyone who dies,' declares the Lord God. 'Therefore, repent and live.'"
> Ezekiel 18:31-32 (Heb. 12:1, 2)

--Notes--

--Notes--

Discovering Ezekiel

For God so loved the world that he gave his only begotten son.... Jn. 3:16

Lesson Ten

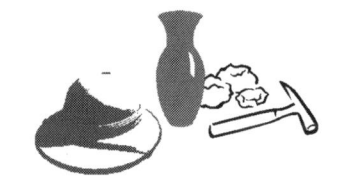

The Desire of My Eyes

What is the *desire of your eyes*? Name at least one thing.

Questions: Ezekiel 24:15-24

1. In Ezekiel 24:15, who is God talking to? _____
2. What did God say He was going to do?

3. In Ezekiel 24:17, what was Ezekiel not to do? _____
4. In verse 18, what happened?

5. Did Ezekiel obey God? _____
6. What did the people ask Ezekiel in verse 19, when they saw that he wasn't mourning his beloved?

7. Why do you think God chose to do something this apparently horrible to innocent Ezekiel?

8. In verse 21-25, what was the symbol that the death of Ezekiel's wife represented?

9. Ezekiel lost his wife, Aaron lost two sons (Lev. 10:1-6), and Job lost all his children (Job 1:18, 19). What do you think the survivors had to learn while suffering from the loss of their loved ones?

10. What did Jesus have to say about our relationship with loved ones in Matthew 10:37-39?

(continued next page)

11. How do you think that Luke 12:16-21 compares with the Israelites' pride in their heritage, country, and children?

12. Think about all the things in this world that you find delightful, that are your pride and joy. Are they more important to you than God is? If so, what could you do to change things before God has to teach you a lesson? (think of Matt. 6:33; 23:37-38)

10 The Desire of My Eyes

God knows what it means to make sacrifices for others. God loved the world so much that He gave up His well-loved son to a horrible death to save others—the son who was the apple of His eye. Jesus.

Sacrificial love.

After God became Ezekiel's personal mentor, while Ezekiel lived as a slave in a foreign land, God spent time teaching him about sacrificial love. This love is None-of-Self and All-of-God. Nothing belonged to Ezekiel on this earth, not even his wife. The second we latch onto anything belonging to this earth and claim it for ourselves, we shove God out the door. Ezekiel learned that not even people are more important than obeying God. He learned to realize that he could not even claim his beloved wife as his own, because God possessed her; and when God took her away, he wanted to not only teach Ezekiel, but to also show the other Israelites living in the area that he had also taken away *the apple of their eyes*: their freedom, their pride, their homeland, their temple, and everything else they cherished.

> What is the apple, the desire, of your eye?

Even Jesus understood this when He obeyed God by voluntarily giving up His glorious existence in heaven to become a human in the flesh. Jesus laid His desires deep into the concrete base of pleasing God. What about you and me?

My job is God's. My house, my spouse, my kids, my hobbies, my pets, my body, my life are God's property. Most of all, my religion belongs to God. I have no more say in how religion should operate, than I do with anything else in this world. The Israelite leaders had to also learn this lesson, because the reason Babylon held them in captivity was because the Jewish leaders had changed and corrupted God's religion, mixing it with the practices of world-religion.

Jesus summed it all up quite effectively, by saying, "You shall love the Lord your God with all your heart, and with all your soul, and with all your mind. This is the great and foremost commandment," (Matt. 22:37-38).

To please the Living God, we must stop letting our eyes rove around the world and allowing the temporary things in the world to distract us, and stop desiring the pretty baubles called "the desires of the flesh, the desires of the eyes, and the pride if life" (1 Jn. 2:15-17; Mt. 10:37). Our eyes, thoughts, and mind must learn, instead, how to desire God's righteousness, how to desire God's Son, and how to desire God's words, God's will, and God's home (Col. 3:1-10).

What do your eyes desire?

--Notes--

...in every nation the man who fears him and does what is right, is acceptable to him. Acts 10:35

Discovering Ezekiel

Lesson Eleven

Sooner or Later
Ezekiel 25-32

1. Read the following verses in order, and then comment on what you think the theme is in this collection: John 1:46; John 4:9; John 7:52; Acts 10:28, 34, 35; Jonah 3:1-10; 4:6-11

2. Were the Gentiles as loved by God as the Israelites were? _____

3. Write down the names of the nations that God judges in Ezekiel, chapters 25-32 (look at topic titles)

    a)   e)

    b)   f)

    c)   g)

    d)

In this lesson, we'll study only Edom, Tyre, and Egypt.

4. Ezekiel 25:13; 35:3, 4-9; and Jeremiah 49:13, 17…What will God do to Edom?

5. Why did God plan on destroying Edom?

    a. Ezek. 25:12 _____

    b. Ezek. 35:5, 6 _____

    c. Ezek. 35:12, 13 _____

    d. Ezek. 35:15 _____

6. Ezekiel 26:3-5; 26:12-14, 21…What will God do to Tyre?

7. Why did God plan on destroying Tyre?

    e. Ezek. 28:2 _____

    f. Ezek. 28:5 _____

    g. Ezek. 28:16 _____

    h. Ezek. 28:17 _____

    i. Ezek. 28:18 _____

(continued next page)

8. Ezekiel 29:10-12, 14-16; 30:24…What will God do to Egypt?

9. Why did God plan on punishing Egypt?
    j. Ezek. 29:3 _____
    k. Ezek. 29:6-7 _____

10. In each case of judgment, God had the same root reason for judging these people:
    l. Ezek. 26:6 _____
    m. Ezek. 29:9 _____
    n. Ezek. 35:4 _____

11. What does the word *Lord* actually mean and what does the significance of its meaning have to do with question 7, above?

12. God totally destroyed and wiped out Edom, Tyre, Moab, and the Philistines. Why do you think that God did not totally destroy Egypt?

Did God actually keep His promises?

Edom: In 600 BC, Jeremiah prophesied against Edom. In 500 BC, Ezekiel prophesied against Edom, too. In 300 AD, the King's Highway shifted from going through Edom to, instead, go through the city of Palmyra. In 632 AD, Edom's city of Petra was destroyed by Mohammedans and it disappeared. In 1188 AD, the Saracens left Teman and Dedan in ruins. Petra was discovered in 1812 and their state of preservation still astonishes archeologists.

Tyre: Ezekiel prophesied against it in 550 BC. In 586 BC, Nebuchadnezzar laid it under siege for thirteen years, and the defendants moved to an island, while their once beautiful city lay in ruins. In 322 BC, Alexander the Great made a causeway out of the old city to reach the island, and he destroyed the newer city. Now, only fishermen work their nets there, as Ezekiel foretold.

Egypt: Ezekiel said it would never again reach preeminence in the world, and it has not.

11 Sooner or Later

Humility and right actions open the way into success for any nation, whether a nation believes in Jehovah God, or not. When countries begin to think more highly of themselves than they ought to, then they start down the path of guaranteed self-destruction. The people of Israel, many times, latched onto this proud, arrogant attitude; and each time, God shoved them to their knees, pressing their faces to the ground, in order to teach them humility. Finally tiring of it, God totally wiped out the northern half of the kingdom, using the Assyrians, and later He destroyed the southern half of the kingdom, using the Babylonians (Is. 5:25-29). Apparently, though, a nation does not need to be "the people of God" in order for God to teach them humility.

God's reason for bringing any nation to ruin, or for utterly wiping them off the face of the earth, or for bringing them under the control of another nation, has always centered around the fact that He is the one true God (Ex. 14-16). What a simple basis. The ideas of humility, of long term success, and of knowing that Jehovah is the only Master, all seem to work together as a one package deal.

Evidently, when a nation loses its sense of right and wrong and grows puffed up in performing sinful sexual deeds, violence, and hateful acts, then that nation has lost its senses. "By righteousness a nation is lifted up, but sin is a cause of shame to the peoples (Pro. 14:34)." People like to think that their sinful abilities are a matter of pride, but in actuality, they are shameful (Eph. 5:11, 12). Sooner or later, God will teach any group of people the difference between arrogance and humility.

In Ezekiel's book of prophecy, he devotes the last few chapters in telling several nations surrounding Judah that because of their sinful practices and self-pride, God would punish them. Some nations God planned to erase, others would become ruins, some He would schedule humility lessons for them and He would not allow them world importance again, and He would punish others for just a short time before allowing them to once again have importance in the world. God actually calls all those nations by their names, even talking about their different histories, and it did not matter that those nations did not claim Him as their deity.

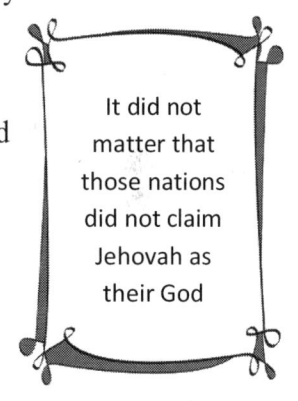

> It did not matter that those nations did not claim Jehovah as their God

Many examples outside of the book of Ezekiel talk about God interacting with different nations. For example, in the book of Jonah we have the story of God warning the extremely proud and violently cruel people of Assyria, the most powerful nation in the world at that time. God had raised them up to punish His people and other wicked nations in that area, but sooner or later, Assyria herself wrote her own name on God's list of Needing-To-Be-Punished. God had enough mercy on them to send Jonah to tell them to change their sinful ways or He would soon destroy them. The Assyrians listened to Jonah and changed their lifestyles immediately, which led to their salvation. Many years later, the Assyrians again forgot how to practice righteousness, and God finally wiped them totally off the face of the earth; and nobody knew for sure that they ever existed at all until, in 1842, somebody stumbled onto their ruins under some hills in northern Iraq, near the city of modern day Mosul. What a humbling experience for such a powerful nation!

God doesn't just blow a country away with His own breath, or a twitch of His little finger, although He could (2 Ki. 19:35). God usually raises up other nations to do the job for Him! For example, He used a righteous nation, Israel, to bring judgment against the Canaanites in Joshua's day. Then, when the Israelites turned wicked and proud, God used nations like Moab, Edom, Phoenicia, Canaan, Syria, Egypt, and others to humble them in return. It's like watching a children's see-saw plank in action, one side going up while the other goes down, back and forth, until someone stops the cycle. In Isaiah 5:25-29, God explains how He does this process, "He will raise a signal for nations far away, and whistle for them from the ends of the earth; and behold, quickly, speedily they come!" The Lord then explains how those other nations come, all excited, healthy, strong, ready to fight, plunder, kill, and oh, so very willing to make the effort in traveling the long distances. God generally brings the worst, or the cruelest, of the nations in to punish a country (Ez. 7:24). Then in Isaiah 11:12, the Lord explains how He'll raise his own people back up, by giving them the same signal, and by making them powerful again. This never-ending cycle happened over and over during Bible times, and the same cycle has kept up the grind all the way into our time.

What we have a hard time realizing, is that God has His own armory! He has His own weapons to use against people who align themselves against righteousness (Jer. 50:25). No amount of strutting, showing off soldiers, tanks, airplanes, or bombs, will help once God puts on His own fighting outfit, because whatever God has will be way bigger than anything man has put together (Jer. 51:53). God is the one who brings on the destruction of nations, peoples, groups, and individuals. God is the one who causes nations to fight against each other (Rev. 6:3). I mean, remember the Tower of Babel in Genesis? He doesn't want man to have the ability to band together as one unit—ever again! The invention of diverse languages and cultures came from Jehovah God himself. This one thing has caused strife among different groups of people ever since the days of that Tower, not counting all the other reasons out there in which to start a good fight.

> God has his own armory of weapons, and he knows how to use it!

Getting back to humility, when a nation gets too proud and forgets that it came from nothing in the first place, and thinks it is better than everybody else, doing whatever it wants to do in evil deeds, then the One who raised that country up in the first place, sooner or later, will slap it down. God did the same thing with Nebuchadnezzar, king of Babylon, raising him up in fame and power, and then when Nebuchadnezzar forgot who dwelt as the real power in the universe, God humbled him with mental illness, the insane behavior of a wild beast, that lasted quite some time (Dan.4). When God allowed the king to come back to his senses and to his throne, Nebuchadnezzar said, "I, Nebuchadnezzar, praise and extol and honor the King of heaven, for all is works are right and his ways are just; and those who walk in pride he is able to humble (Dan. 4:37)."

In conclusion, God knows every hair on each person's head, and He knows everyone's thoughts and intentions, and He knows every nation, and He knows the humble and the proud, from the great to the insignificant. The Lord also sets up the leaders of nations and He takes them down (Rom. 13:1). God promises that He will tear down the "house of the proud" and that He hates the arrogant (Prov. 15:25; 21:4; 16:5). "Humble yourselves before the Lord, and he will exalt you," which are fitting words from the half-brother of Jesus Christ, who at one time had to learn humility before his own brother, Jesus (Jas. 4:10).

--Notes--

--Notes--

Discovering Ezekiel

For the wages of sin is death, but the free gift of God is eternal life in Christ Jesus our Lord.
Rom. 6:23

Lesson Twelve

The Grand Revival
Ezekiel 36:21-38; 37

Questions:

1. What do the words *restore* and *renew* mean (use the dictionary)?

2. What was God's main concern about in Ezekiel 36:21 and 22? _____

3. For who's sake was God going to *act* according to verse 22, and why?

4. Through the rest of chapter 36, what exactly was this action, or this vindication, going to be?

5. Did you ever treat someone bad and they treated you good in return, forgiving you in spite of what you did? Talk about verse 31, in describing your feelings about yourself during a situation like that.

6. When you read verses 21-38, what comparison(s) do you find in this passage with the word *restoration*?

7. In Ezekiel 37:1-10, what exactly happened to Ezekiel and what did he see?

8. What was God's explanation for this vision, in verses 11-14?

(continued next page)

67

9. How does this explanation compare with our Christian lives? (2 Tim. 1:10; Gal. 2:20; Rom. 6:6-11; John 11:25-26; John 10:10; 1 Cor. 15:50-58)

10. So, what would being *renewed* and being *restored* mean to you in your life?

12   The Grand Revival

Raising the dead to life, both spiritually and physically, proves to be God's most favorite hobby. He must have relished showing the prophet Ezekiel the fantastic vision of dry, human bones coming to life in Ezekiel 36. God created a masterly production of a supernaturally weird experience, just like our ultra-modern science fictions or fantasy movies.

A mass of human skeletons plugged up an immense valley, where God took Ezekiel in a vision. He plopped the Israelite priest down smack in the middle of this monstrous scene of horror. Then, the Lord told Ezekiel to stand there, face the bones, and preach. Just think about it for a second. God told this human to preach to millions of bones that couldn't hear anything. Well, Ezekiel obeyed, and while he preached, he saw the skeletons gradually reform themselves into human bodies, sinew by sinew, organ by organ. Then God ordered him to preach the breath into them. Ezekiel kept preaching and suddenly saw the bodies began to move and then stand up. They lived! He now stood in the middle of thousands of people who had been nothing a few minutes before!

Ezekiel discovered God's passion, making something out of nothing, transforming horror into joy, bringing the dead to life with just His words! God's words alone, preached from man's tongue, can bring life into the calcified dead.

> Ezekiel discovered God's great passion!

"But God being rich in mercy because of his great love with which he loved us, *even when we were dead in our transgressions, made us alive together with Christ* (by grace you have been saved), and *raised us up* with him, and seated us with him in the heavenly places, in Christ Jesus, in order that in the ages to come *he might show the surpassing riches of his grace* in kindness toward us in Christ Jesus," (Eph. 2:4-7).

Through the ages, God has had mercy on people, in order to display His own glory and His own greatness, not ours. This poses a problem for most, since we want to be the ones glorified and famous, and many times we find it impossible to humble ourselves and let the glory go to God. Therefore, we literally and figuratively, remain as helpless, gross, dry bones scattered in unknown valleys, instead of being alive in Christ, where we can find all blessings and riches (Eph. 1:3).

A great example of God's passion for renewing life shows up in the apostle Paul. As Saul in his younger life, he and his Friend-Skeletons caused havoc and misery for the people who believed in Jesus —killing them, throwing them in prison, and seizing their property. One day, God slammed down on Saul and his cronies with a light-force and with His words, and God began knitting Saul together again with flesh, organs, a heart, and a mind (Acts 9). Then God brought to Saul a man named Ananias (like the man Ezekiel) whom God told to preach the breath into Saul. Saul was born-again in watery baptism and Saul gradually became known as Paul. Paul became a God's-Word-Breathing-Man after that moment. The rest of us do not have that option of God slamming down on us with His light-force. He did it once with Paul. He did it with Noah. He did it with Mary and Joseph. He did it with Cornelius. We now have it in God's Word, the Bible. The words in the Bible are enough to knit us into real people, with real lives.

Most humans have a tendency of choosing to live a lifeless, dry-bone-life, instead of living, moving, and having our being in the God who has such a rich imagination for turning nothing into something (Acts 17:28). Placing ourselves in the hands of the supernatural God is always an exciting life. He never allows us to get bored. If we ever get tired of being Christians, then we cannot blame God. If we find ourselves indifferent or turned off to doing things that please God, then we have jumped out of His protective hand, and we have allowed ourselves to return to lying around in a bone-choked valley—just some dry bones lost among millions of other dry bones.

Please, don't allow yourself to get into this situation! Live the Christian life as Paul suggests by renewing your soul daily, and daily making sure of your calling which God called you, and daily placing your soul in God's very capable hands, and Live! (Rom. 12:1, 2; Eph. 4:11, Jn. 10:10).

--Notes--

THE AUTHOR

Tam Raynor has spent much of her life studying the Bible, teaching classes, attending lectureships and classes, worshiping God, listening to thousands of sermons, and reading many religious and spiritual books. She graduated from Lubbock Christian University with a BA in Art, and then graduated from National University in Southern California with a Master's Degree in Secondary Education. Her husband, Chris, decided to become a preacher, and after graduating from Brown Trail School of Preaching, in Ft. Worth, Texas, they became missionaries in Tanzania for several years. At the time of this book publishing, Chris preaches for the Church of Christ in Northeast, Ohio.

If you find any problems, errors, or type-o's in this book, please feel free to smirk and feel superior, because Tam has edited this umpteen times and now retires.

Made in the USA
Columbia, SC
11 June 2025